KU-009-194

To Alfie William

to celebrate the birth

of his cousins Joseph

and Lily on 7.2.05

Love

Nanny + Grandad

xx

God's Special Prayer

Marjory Francis
and Helen Jenkins

Copyright © Marjory Francis 2004
First published 2004
ISBN 1 84427 054 8

Scripture Union, 207–209 Queensway,
Bletchley, Milton Keynes, MK2 2EB, England.
Email: info@scriptureunion.org.uk
Website: www.scriptureunion.org.uk

Scripture Union Australia
Locked Bag 2, Central Coast Business Centre,
NSW 2252
Website: www.su.org.au

Scripture Union USA
PO Box 987, Valley Forge, PA 19482
www.scriptureunion.org

All rights reserved. No part of this publication may be reproduced,
stored in a retrieval system, or transmitted in any form or by any
means, electronic, mechanical, photocopying, recording or otherwise,
without the prior permission of Scripture Union.

The right of Marjory Francis to be identified as author of this work has
been asserted by her in accordance with the Copyright, Designs and
Patents Act 1988.

The Lord's Prayer, as it appears in Common Worship: Service and
Prayers for the Church of England (Church House Publishing 2000),
is copyright © The English Language Liturgical Consultation and is
reproduced by permission of the publisher.

British Library Cataloguing-in-Publication Data.

A catalogue record of this book is available from the British Library.

Printed and bound in Singapore by Tien Wah Press.

Design: kwgraphicdesign

Cover and all internal illustrations: Helen Jenkins

Scripture Union is an international Christian charity
working with churches in more than 130 countries.

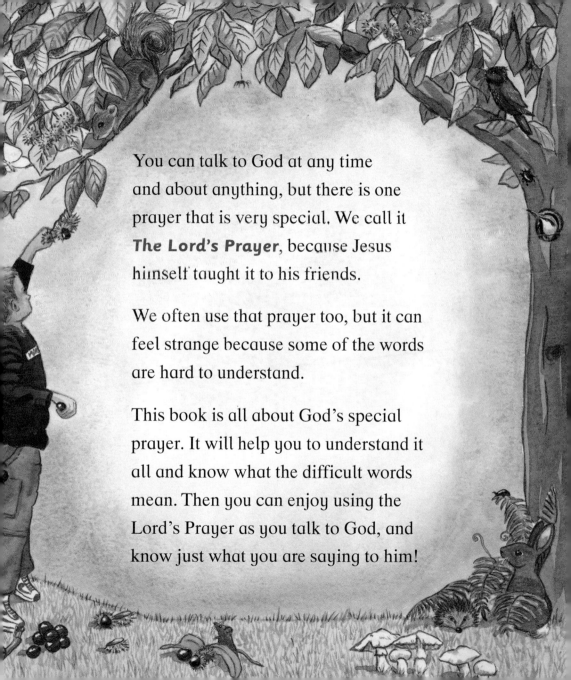

You can talk to God at any time and about anything, but there is one prayer that is very special. We call it **The Lord's Prayer**, because Jesus himself taught it to his friends.

We often use that prayer too, but it can feel strange because some of the words are hard to understand.

This book is all about God's special prayer. It will help you to understand it all and know what the difficult words mean. Then you can enjoy using the Lord's Prayer as you talk to God, and know just what you are saying to him!

When
you make
something it is
special to you. God has made
everything! We can't see him, but
he is a great Father who loves and
cares for everything he has made,
and that means us too!

Our Father in heaven

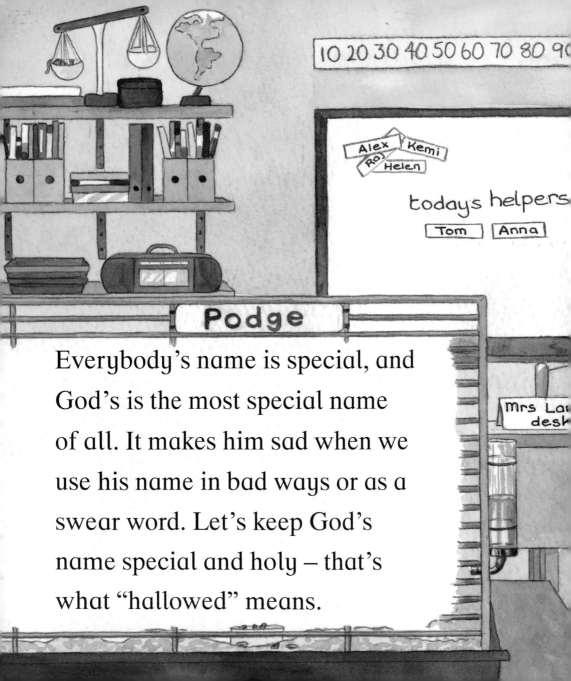

10 20 30 40 50 60 70 80 90

Alex Kemi
Raj
Helen

today's helpers

Tom   Anna

Podge

mrs Lar
desk

Everybody's name is special, and God's is the most special name of all. It makes him sad when we use his name in bad ways or as a swear word. Let's keep God's name special and holy – that's what "hallowed" means.

hallowed be your name

Jesus didn't dress like a king when he lived on earth, but he showed us what a good king is like. In God's kingdom no one will be sad or hurt or unkind. We want to help God's kingdom come on earth too.

your kingdom come

God always knows what's best
for us – he wants us to be
happy! It's not always easy to
see that God's way is best, but
he will help us as we pray
"your will be done."

your will be done,
on earth as in heaven.

Give us today our daily bread.

Every day we have good things to eat. God has made sure enough food grows in the world for everyone. Remember to thank him, and to pray for the people who don't get their fair share.

Sometimes we do wrong things
and need to say sorry to the
people or person we have hurt
and to God. God is always
ready to forgive us!

Forgive us our sins

When someone has done
something wrong to us
we need to be ready to
forgive them.

Sometimes that
can be very hard!

as we forgive those
who sin against us.

Lead us not into temptation

Sometimes doing wrong looks fun, but we will always feel unhappy inside afterwards. We need God's help to say "no" when we are tempted to do wrong.

Everyone can be frightened, and sometimes people can be in danger. When this happens it is good to remember that Jesus is close by, loving and caring for us.

but deliver us from evil.

God is so great
and wonderful, it is
difficult to describe him. We
just want to say "God you're
great! And we're so glad that
we can live with you for ever!"

For the kingdom, the power and the glory are yours, now and for ever.

Amen.

When you join in "Amen", you are saying "I agree with what has been said. This is my prayer too!"